Opting For The Poor:
A Challenge For North Americans

Peter J Henriot, S.J.

Center of Concern
Washington, D.C.
1990

362
439

c.2

DEDICATION

To the team at the Center of Concern who have enriched
my understanding of the indirect option for the poor.

To the neighbors of K Street who have challenged my practice
of the direct option for the poor.

To the Jesuits of the Center and K Street who have supported me in both
options by word and example.

ACKNOWLEDGEMENTS

I want to thank the Columban Fathers, USA, the Giving Fund of the Central Province of the Missionary Oblates of Mary Immaculate and the Justice and Peace Fund of the Dominican Sisters of Racine, for their generous assistance toward the publication of this book.

Many persons have contributed to the writing of this book. My life has been especially touched by the poor of Washington, D.C. and other Third World areas. I am grateful to the participants of numerous workshops I've offered over the years on this topic. They have challenged my thinking and shared their own experiences. I owe a special debt of gratitude to Dean Brackley, S.J., and Jim Hug, S.J., who provided me with very valuable editorial suggestions. Jim Hug, Sylvia Diss and Judy Mladineo have seen the manuscript through to its published form and for this help I am deeply appreciative.

Series Preface

t the beginning of the cosmos: the unleashing of unbelievable energy. Energy expanding through space and periods of time that stretch the limits of human imagining. Energy, the dynamism of life, generating creativity and hope. Energy, the vibrant soul of all that is and is becoming. An active name for God. Human history and contemporary society are the legacy of the convergences and clashes of these energies. How can the energies, flowing within us, around us, among us, be guided to create a more liberating, just and loving human community–the kind of world Jesus and the women and men who shared community with him envisioned when they spoke of the coming of the Reign of God? That question is at the heart of this series of small books from the CENTER OF CONCERN.

ENERGIES FOR SOCIAL TRANSFORMATION is being designed to help individuals and groups get in touch with the deepest human/divine energies within them, among them, around them in society, We hope it will facilitate the discernment of the action and call of God and free those energies for the task of social transformation required if God is to reign more fully over human life and we are to know a societal life graced with greater justice and love.

Social transformation for a more just society is a massive undertaking. We have watched the energy and commitment to change that set the 1960s on fire in the U.S. co-opted or bottled up in the frustration and disillusionment of the 1970s, dissolving all too often into cynical disillusionment in the 1980s. Conspicuous radicals of the 60s have emerged as establishment neo-conservatives in the 80s, speaking of their 'conversions' and praising the system that is now treating them so well. Even those who did not succumb to such 'conversions' saw many in their ranks suffer burnout. Through these decades the realization has gradually grown that institutional social change not grounded in cultural renewal is too shallow. The myths, the values, the images, the hopes, the dreams of a people - these give guidance to human energies. If the injustices they embody are not cleansed, if they are not broken open and reshaped, societal progress will continue to be undermined and eroded like the biblical mansion built on sand.

The Reign of God demands both institutional and cultural transformation. That overwhelming challenge can only be taken up in any sustained way by people who can draw upon the energies, rootedness, and staying power of communities of faith. Rich community life is essential for providing the love and cohesion essential for true conversion, creative revisioning and faithful commitment to social transformation in the spirit of Jesus. The Second Vatican Council generated an important renewal of faith, community life, and Christian spirituality which have begun to give birth to this essential context. There have been some serious limitations in this renewal, however, limitations that must be overcome if the energies of God flowing within and among us are to be really liberated to serve the emergence of God's Reign in society. In the renewal in spirituality flowing out of the Council, for example, the principal channels of growth have been opened by psychology. Psychological insights have opened our eyes in remarkable ways to God's presence and movement in the emotional energies of our interior lives. But they have been far less successful in helping us meet and be renewed by the God of political and economic, social and cultural life who was the heart and focus of Israel's faith. This limitation has unwittingly re-enforced the Enlightenment compartmentalization of life that has locked Christian faith in the realm of private life. The God of unbounded cosmic energy, however, will not be domesticated. We are being called to liberate our faith energies, to reintegrate in a single faith vision all of our life commitments, all dimensions of personal and social life. ENERGIES FOR SOCIAL TRANSFORMATION hopes to nurture that reintegration.

Another significant discovery during the post-Vatican II renewal has been the gradual realization that the experience and energies of some groups have been overlooked, ignored, rejected as insignificant. The women of the world are among these

groups. So are the poor. God's Reign
cannot be whole until they are liberated
and integral participants in a just and loving
human community. Volumes in this series
are designed to enable their voices to be
heard and their energies liberated for the
social transformation that is needed to
redeem us all.

It is ironic that in an era when we
know more about the energies of the
cosmos than ever before and when we
can release and guide more power than
ever before, our culture engenders so much
passivity and paralysis. ENERGIES FOR
SOCIAL TRANSFORMATION is offered as a
help to breaking out of that paralysis, to
discovering the divine energies moving in
society, and to entering with compassionate
justice and fierce love into the redeeming of
the earth.

Table of Contents

Was I like the priest or levite in the parable of the Good Samaritan, rushing by a needy person on the side of the road in order to attend some important business?

Introduction

Several years ago, I was rushing to the Rayburn House Office Building in Washington, D.C., to attend a morning meeting to discuss legislation dealing with domestic and global hunger. As usual, I was late. Cutting through the park in front of Union Station, about two blocks from the Capitol, I moved quickly past a middle-aged woman who was leaning against a lamp post. She was poorly dressed and looked quite forlorn. Used to the many street people in the area, I didn't pay much attention to her, except to notice that she seemed particularly sad. For just a moment, I thought about stopping to see if I could help her. But the importance of the meeting I was hurrying to propelled me forward and away from personal contact.

A few minutes later, sitting in one of the grand rooms of the Rayburn Building, I found myself unable to concentrate on the presentation being made on the plight of the hungry and on the policies needed to meet the problem. The image of that woman kept returning to haunt me and raise disturbing questions. Had I ignored a hungry person in order to discuss hunger? Was I like the priest or levite in the parable of the Good Samaritan, rushing by a needy person on the side of the road in order to attend to some important business? I've never forgotten that woman, though I've had occasion to see many more poor persons just like her in conditions as bad or much worse. And I've still not learned the exactly appropriate response to the needs of the poor. I continue to feel the tension between responding to the immediate needs of the poor and working for the social change necessary to deal with the structures of poverty. I know that I'm not alone in experiencing that tension.

This small book on the option for the poor is an attempt to deal better with that tension. I'm convinced that my response as a Christian in North America today has to be on both levels: meeting the poor as persons and dealing with the structures of poverty. Opting for the poor requires the personal and the structural.

My seventeen years in Washington with the Center of Concern have given me wonderful opportunities to learn from others. I readily acknowledge and thank those who helped me grow in an under-standing of and response to the option for the poor. Travelling and living in the Third World of Latin America, Asia, and Africa, and Third World of inner-city Washington, D.C. and other parts of North America have opened my eyes and touched my heart. The McKenna Center shelter and the soup kitchen of SOME (So Others Might Eat) have given me a chance to be with the poor. Groups like Interfaith Action for

Economic Justice and the Coalition for a New Foreign Policy have enabled me to work for the structural change needed to promote justice in our nation and world.

This book has been in the making for a long time. After innumerable lectures and workshops, dozens of articles, and several video and audio tapes, I'm finally putting my thoughts on this topic into a more organized and complete presentation. Yet I'll be the first to admit that much more needs to be said about the option for the poor, certainly more than I'm able to say at this time.

Of course, it is also true that much more needs to be *done* about the option for the poor. That's something we can all be about. Less talk and more action will make the option both clearer and more effective. For this reason, I've tried to write this book in as practical a fashion as possible. At times my style is more conversational than usual, because I'm trying to share insights, experiences, and calls, while inviting you, the reader, to do the same. Together we need to move forward in opting for the poor.

This book is obviously written for the non-poor. It is intended for a variety of uses. It can be reflected on privately or in groups. The six chapters could be the basis for a six-week post-RENEW program or similar adult discussion groups. Study questions and scriptural references are designed to promote further reflection, prayer and action.

CHAPTER 1

*"Our God hears the cry of the poor.
Blessed be our God!"*

Challenging
Our Church

We have sung that song many times in recent years. At liturgies. At special prayer services. In demonstrations. In workshops.

Our God does hear the cry of the poor — we know that. But do we? That is the serious question, the critical challenge, which faces our church today. Do we really hear the cry of the poor? That is the issue behind the phrase "the option for the poor."

In the language of our Christian community, certain words and phrases frequently catch a mood, an emphasis, an issue, which is important at a particular moment of the church's development. In the task of sharing the Good News, these words and phrases sum up a faith dimension especially appropriate to the time.

For example, "Mystical Body" was a popular way of describing the church in the years before the Second Vatican Council. Since then, we are more familiar with the phrase "People of God," emphasizing the actual community in history. "Catholic

Action" described the involvement of the laity in the church's mission years ago; today, "lay ministry" is a more common and appropriate expression. For many Catholics, "evangelization" still sounds a little "Protestant," and yet it is fast becoming a very good Catholic word — and action!

Recently, we have heard the phrases "preferential option for the poor" and "solidarity with the poor" used in discussions of the church's mission. For many of us in North America, the phrases have a foreign ring to them, sounding like something imported from Latin America. For others, the phrases seem offensive and liable to create division in the church.

When the U.S. Catholic bishops used the phrase "preferential option for the poor" in the first draft of their 1986 Pastoral Letter, Economic Justice for All: Catholic Social Teaching and the U.S. Economy, they were sharply attacked by critics who accused them of introducing dangerous ideas. Many objected that the phrase was out of place in a U.S. church document. Didn't it have radical, even Marxist, overtones? There were strong pressures to drop it altogether.

Yet to their credit the bishops kept the phrase, developing further its meaning in the subsequent drafts of the Economic Pastoral. They nuanced and strengthened the theme, making it clear that it belongs to the world church and flows from the radical message of the Gospel.

TENSIONS

But to be honest, "option for the poor" continues to be an expression easily subject to misunderstanding. And it is not a topic which is readily discussed. Emotions tend to run high when it is introduced into conversations. Why is this so? There seem to be tensions both around the meaning of the phrase and around its implications.

The tensions around meaning arise mainly from a lack of clarity. Who are the poor? Why are they poor? What does it mean to "opt for" the poor? What about those of us who do not work directly with the poor? Can we have this option? Should we? Why should this be so important today? Is it just a passing fad? Tomorrow, will we have an "option for the middle class"? There are usually as many different

Homeless people roam city streets in tattered clothing...

answers to these questions are there are persons involved in the debate.

But there are also tensions around implications. These arise from fears of what this option may require of us. What are we being challenged to do? What judgments are being made on what we have been doing in the past? What might we have to change? To give up? Should we feel "guilty" about the situations of the poor? How political are we called to be by this option? The implications sometimes appear to be more than many of us care to pursue.

Over the years, I've found much more heat than light in conversations on this topic. More than any other dimension of the church's mission today, it seems able to divide, frustrate, paralyze. Even when people feel deeply the blessings which come from being on the side of the poor, the consequences for the whole church — its ministry, style, priorities, possessions — seem illusive, contradictory, frightening. This is an experience, I believe, that is shared not only by Christians in North America but by Christians throughout the world.

Some time ago, I participated in an international meeting of Jesuits, reviewing our recent history of mission and planning for the future. Overall, it was an exciting and basically energizing event for me. But I remember quite distinctly that whenever the topics of "option for the poor" or "solidarity with the poor" or "vow of poverty" or "simplicity of life style" arose, a terrible depression would come over the group. We seemed able to discuss almost any other topic quite readily, even those of considerable controversy such as dissent within the church. But "option for the poor" definitely frightened us! In a traditional "discernment of spirits," it was evident that our discomfort, moodiness, anger were all clear signs of a desolation that revealed a much deeper issue.

What is that deeper issue? It seems to me that it is simply our closeness to Jesus today, Jesus in the poor. To take seriously the call to make an option for the poor, touches the deepest chords in our faith and challenges the most established patterns in our culture. It calls us to engage in a profound struggle in our day. It's no

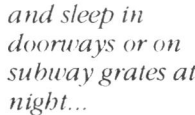

and sleep in doorways or on subway grates at night...

wonder that tension can arise so readily when the topic is raised!

CONTEXT

We don't look at the topic of the preferential option for the poor in a vacuum. We are in a specific historical context. And the most significant element in the context of our present discussions about the option for the poor is simply the fact of the poor. A national and global fact. A tragic and inescapable fact.

The United States, one of the richest countries in the world, is the home of millions of poor. These poor live in urban and rural areas, are women and men, young and old, employed and unemployed, and of many different ethnic and racial backgrounds.

Over thirty million people in the United States are poor according to the official government definition. This is fifteen per cent of our population. Each day they lack sufficient diet, live in inadequate housing, and miss out on basic medical care. One in four children under the age of six in this country is poor, one in two black children. In fact, a higher proportion of U.S. children live in poverty than do children in West Germany, Britain, Canada and several other industrial democracies.

An increasing number of the poor in the United States are women and those dependent on women — the phenomenon of the "feminization of poverty." More than 10 percent of white U.S. citizens currently live below the poverty line. But 33.1 percent of Black citizens and 28.2 percent of Hispanics are poor.

When the U.S. Catholic bishops spoke of poverty and its increase in this country in recent years, they said:

As pastors we have seen firsthand the faces of poverty in our midst. Homeless people roam city streets in tattered clothing and sleep in doorways or on subway grates at night. Many of these are former mental patients released from state hospitals. Thousands stand in line at soup kitchens because they have no other way of feeding themselves. Millions of children are so poorly nourished that their physical and mental development are seriously harmed (#172).

The global situation of poverty is well known, perhaps too well known. We all too frequently have become numbed by the numbers: of the five billion people alive today, almost one billion live below a line of extreme poverty and another two billion live close to that line. We speak often of the "Third World." Really, it is the "Two-thirds World" — the majority of our human family.

Forty thousand people a day die of hunger and malnutrition — one every two seconds. Most of these are children. Millions of people are refugees, living on the run or settling in squalid camps. Unemployment and underemployment devastate lives and break up families. Illiteracy stifles creativity.

The Economic Pastoral bluntly reminds us that the misery of the global poor "is not the inevitable result of the march of history or of the intrinsic nature of particular cultures, but of human decisions and human institutions" (#254). The tragedy is that we have the economic and technical resources to meet the world's problems but we seem to lack the political and moral resources to act on behalf of the poor.

REFLECTION

Television has brought vivid images of domestic and global poverty into homes throughout North America. But the television coverage of famine in Ethiopia or homelessness in Washington, DC can be interrupted by pet food commercials or simply turned off by the dulled and frustrated viewer. The reality of poverty goes relentlessly on, however. And the response of the option for the poor becomes increasingly urgent.

The church is challenged severely by this option for the poor, in its identity and its mission. The U.S. bishops acknowledged this in a particularly strong statement in the Economic Pastoral:

No one can claim the name Christian and be comfortable in the face of the hunger, homelessness, insecurity and injustice found in this country and the world. (#27)

However we may feel about the proper personal or political response to the problems of poverty, it is clear that the preferential option for the poor is central to the future of our church.

CHAPTER II

The Judeo Christian tradition is marked by a profound concern for the poor, identification with their suffering, and solidarity with their struggles.

Tracing the History

One of the common defenses against the unsettling dimensions of the call for the option for the poor is the argument that this option is a novelty, something of a fad. Why all this fuss about something that has only recently been stressed in the practice of our Christian faith? If the church got along for many centuries without this emphasis, why introduce it now, especially since it seems to divide the community? What is the history of this option for the poor?

Historical questions are good questions. They provoke us to probe deeper, to rediscover rich traditions which may have been overlooked. This challenge to the current stress on the preferential option for the poor needs a clarifying response, one which sets the theme within an historical perspective.

CHURCH PRACTICE

The option for the poor is not a new fad for the Christian community. The

Judeo-Christian tradition is marked by a profound concern for the poor, identification with their suffering, and solidarity with their struggles. Over the centuries, this concern, identification and solidarity have taken many different forms. I find helpful in this historical discussion a perspective offered by the Canadian theologian, Gregory Baum. Baum suggests five stages in the development of the Christian community's exercise of solidarity with the poor. While there is clearly an historical progression through these stages, obviously today all five are still in evidence.

1. The early Christian community, in continuity with its heritage from Israel, practiced a solidarity with the poor. Those who were not poor shared with the poor, both through communal living and through alms. We see this in the style of the first community: "Those who believed shared all things in common; they would sell their property and goods, dividing everything on the basis of each one's need" (Acts 2: 44-45; see also 4: 32-35). Paul coordinated a special collection for the poor in the church of Jerusalem (see Acts 24: 17; 1 Cor 16: 1-4; 2 Cor 8 and 9). And he reminded the community of the bonds of solidarity which their compassion would bring: "Your plenty at the present time should supply their need so that their surplus may one day supply your need, with equality as a result" (2 Cor 8: 14).

Today the compassionate option for the poor is present in the numerous collections taken up in churches to assist the less fortunate in North America and around the world. In the U.S. Catholic Church, for example, the Campaign for Human Development, Catholic Relief Services, and numerous diocesan programs are designed to share resources with the poor. Almsgiving is still an exercise in the option for the poor.

2. In the early centuries of Christianity, a more spiritualized identification with the poor was practiced by those women and men who retired to the desert to live lives of prayer and penance. This was an ascetical solidarity with the poor. Simplicity was the rule, with only the bare necessities provided for, in an effort to be close to those who were poor. Hospitality was an important mark of this option for the poor.

As this way of life grew, it was the beginning of community life marked by the religious vow of poverty. To be honest, however, not all interpretations of the life of vowed poverty have led to simplicity and closeness to the poor. For many religious communities — in earlier times and today — vowed poverty has had more to do with the legal title to ownership or with obedience to those in authority or with an abstract notion of "doing without," than with actually living close to the poor. But the goal of the ascetical option, however imperfectly practiced, should continue to be an identification with the poor.

3. A missionary solidarity with the poor has marked the church in its outreach to the poor, both in new evangelization projects in what were formerly called "mission lands" and in efforts to "re-evangelize" what were once Christian cultures and countries. Jesus claimed as an essential characteristic of his mission "preaching the good news to the poor" (see Luke 4: 18, and 7: 22). This task has been carried on in the effort of countless Christians who have struggled over the years to bring the Gospel to the poor of the world.

One thinks immediately of the work of missionaries like St. Peter Claver among the black slaves of Latin America. The more contemporary "Mission de France" sent priests into factories and urban slums to be in solidarity with the struggling working class. The missionary option for the poor has put a special focus on reaching the poor and the outcast of society.

4. As the church has refined its pastoral practices in the light of changing conditions — both within the structures and personnel of the church itself and within society at large — a pastoral solidarity with the poor has been developed. This approach makes service to the poor a priority within the project of planning for the best uses of church resources.

Pastoral service takes many forms, of course. But this particular emphasis on the option for the poor would value operations such as shelters, soup kitchens, family services, etc.

5. Finally, there is what today has come to be called a preferential solidarity with the poor. This speaks not so much to how the church relates to the poor in terms of compassion, identification or service, but more to how the church relates to society at large and to the social structures which influence our life. That is, the church joins in solidarity with the poor in the struggle to transform society toward greater justice.

This transformation involves structural change, not simply amelioration of the sufferings of poverty. Justice not charity, surgery not band-aids. This form of the option for the poor involves that "action on behalf of justice and participation in the transformation of the world" which the 1971

Synod of Bishops declared to be "constituitive of the preaching of the Gospel." The option for the poor which involves the solidarity with the poor is where most attention has been paid in recent years, in theory if not always in practice. We will be exploring its various aspects in the chapters that follow.

CHURCH TEACHING

The historical practice of different forms of exercising the option for the poor provides the Christian community with a wonderfully rich experience. This experience is the basis for the message which the church addresses to the larger society about our obligation to be sensitive to the poor and committed to justice. The tradition of the church's social teaching is replete with references to the poor and calls to work for justice. Our faithful following of Jesus demands no less.

This truth is beautifully stated in what I feel is one of the most significant references to the preferential option for the poor, the opening lines of the great final statement of the Second Vatican Council, The Church in the Modern World (Gaudium et Spes):

> The joys and hopes, the sorrows and anxieties, of the women and men of this age, **especially those who are poor or in any way oppressed**, these are the joys and hopes, the sorrows and anxieties, of the followers of Jesus (#1; author emphasis added).

Paul VI reemphasized this particular priority of focus on the poor in his 1971 Call to Action (Octagesima Adveniens). There he spoke of the Gospel instruction in

The Church joins in solidarity with the poor in their struggle toward a more just society.

the "preferential respect due to the poor and the special situation they have in society" (#23). Earlier, John XXIII in his introductory speech at the Council, had spoken of the "desire of the church to be the church of all, but in a special way the church of the poor."

The stress placed by Council and pope was picked up and developed at greater length in the teaching of the church in Latin America. There the phrase "preferential but non-exclusive option for the poor" came into common usage as a result

of the two great gatherings of the Latin American Episcopal Conference (CELAM), in Medellin (1968) and Puebla (1979). These meetings of CELAM addressed the church's pastoral response to the contemporary needs of the continent.

The final documents of Medellin spoke of the need to give "preference to the poorest and most needy sectors and to those segregated for any cause whatsoever ("Poverty," #9). At Puebla, the bishops stated that they wanted to take up once again the position adopted at Medellin, "a clear and prophetic option expressing preference for, and solidarity with, the poor. We affirm the need for conversion on the part of the whole church to a preferential option for the poor, an option aimed at their integral liberation" [1134].

The Latin American bishops linked the option for the poor to the following of Christ and viewed it as a continuing of his mission in today's world.

...the church became more aware of its mission in the service of the poor, the oppressed and the outcast. In this preferential option, which must not be understood as exclusive, the true spirit of the Gospel shines forth.

"When we draw near to the poor in order to accompany them and serve them, we are doing what Christ taught us to do when he became our brother, poor like us. Hence service to the poor is the privileged, though not the exclusive, gauge of our following of Christ" [1145].

The pastoral plans of the church after Medellin and Puebla reveal this orientation and stance. As we know, it has had far-reaching consequences for the life — and death — of Christians throughout Latin America.

John Paul II has picked up the theme of the "preferential but non-exclusive option for the poor" and brought it into the mainstream of the official teaching of the church. He has repeated it in several of his major addresses during his travels in many different parts of the world. Even more important, however, is his explicit inclusion of the option for the poor in his most recent encyclical, The Social Concern of the Church (Sollicitudo Rei Socialis). There he spoke of the option as one of "the characteristic themes and guidelines dealt with by the magisterium in recent years" (#42).

It is important to note that John Paul II chooses to use "love of preference for the poor" instead of "option for the poor" in referring to this fundamental stance. He writes in The Social Concern of the Church:

This is an option or a special form of primacy in the exercise of Christian charity to which the whole tradition of the church bears witness. It affects the life of each Christian inasmuch as he or she seeks to imitate the life of Christ, but it applies equally to our social responsibilities and hence to our manner of living, and to the logical decisions to be made concerning the ownership and use of goods (#42).

The pope here mentions many of the key elements of the option for the poor: imitation of Christ, societal responsibilities, lifestyle, and economic practices. But his choice of "love" over "option" softens the conflict inherent in choosing sides. Since I feel he may thereby weaken the Gospel force of the call here, I will return to this point in the next chapter.

In his teaching, John Paul II is echoing the 1985 Extraordinary Synod in Rome. This gathering had reviewed developments in the church in the twenty years since the end of the Second Vatican Council and had highlighted the graces of renewal which the church had experienced worldwide. According to the final statement of the Synod:

> Following the Second Vatican Council, the church became more aware of its mission in the service of the poor, the oppressed and the outcast. In this preferential option, which must not be understood as exclusive, the true spirit of the Gospel shines forth (#D-6).

The option for the poor has frequently been associated with liberation theology in Latin America. Liberation theologians have helped us understand the close link between God's actions revealed in Jewish and Christian scripture and the on-going struggle of the poor for justice. From their own social experience, not simply as observers but as participants, these theologians have enriched our appreciation of the central role in Christian life and church activity of the option for the poor.

Given this link between liberation theology and the option for the poor, it is especially significant that when Cardinal Joseph Ratzinger made his clarifications about liberation theology, he explicitly mentioned this option and affirmed its proper place in Christian life. In his 1986 statement, he wrote: "...those who are oppressed by poverty are the object of a love of preference on the part of the Church..." (#II-68). Again, the use of "love" rather than "option" deserves our attention in the next chapter.

Several statements from individual bishops or from regional groups of bishops have also utilized the language of the option for the poor. Notable among these are the Canadian bishops, who in a 1983 statement on the economy spoke of this option and the priority of labor over capital as the two principles which are to be used to evaluate all economic policies and structures. In addition, many religious congregations have incorporated this language into their revised constitutions and mission statements. In so doing, they have called their members to a solidarity with the poor which should mark both their ministry and their lifestyle.

REFLECTION

I have described an historical overview of the option for the poor and mentioned the use of the expression by the Second Vatican Council, popes and other church leaders for a very specific purpose. It is important to remind ourselves of the long-standing and universal character of this emphasis on the privileged place of the poor in the church's mission. This is true even though the Christian community has not always lived up to this ideal. But those who would dismiss the option for the poor on the grounds of it being a passing fad of a particular segment of the church have neither been reading history nor following the development of the church's social teaching throughout the world.

The preferential option for the poor is at the center of the church's affirmation of truth. The challenge is to place it also at the center of the church's life.

CHAPTER III

To be poor is to be hungry, to be without decent shelter and clothes, to lack adequate education and health.

Clarifying the Issues

ell, who are the poor, anyway?"

Certainly that is the most vexing question that arises when we start talking about the option for the poor. It sometimes seems to me — and I suspect I'm not alone in this — that more blood, sweat and tears have gone into debates about defining the poor than into actions on behalf of the poor! This accounts for many of the problems around the exercise of the option for the poor in North America. We need some clarifying definitions.

DEFINITIONS

My own reading of the scriptures and of the every-day use of the word provides me with a very clear and simple definition: the poor are the economically disadvantaged, the materially deprived, who as a consequence suffer powerlessness, exploitation and oppression.

To be poor is to be hungry, to be without decent shelter and clothes, to lack

to be poor is to be hungry...

adequate educational and healthcare opportunities, to be unemployed, to be on the margin of society, to feel excluded from decisions that affect you, to feel controlled by outside forces, to be unable to deal with problems of daily existence, to be discriminated against.

But I hear some people challenging me about this definition. Aren't there persons who are economically well off and yet who genuinely experience poverty? Isn't it excessively narrow to concentrate only on material deprivation in speaking of the poor and the option for the poor? What about the spiritually poor — the suburban family with many material blessings but no sense of God in their lives? Or the psychologically poor — the young man in college who has great doubts about his identity and is feeling very lonely? Or the emotionally poor — the career woman who lacks any real love in her life and is becoming addicted to drugs? Or the physically poor — the successful businessman who must contend with a serious handicap?

No, I don't consider these people poor!

I do not think that it is accurate or helpful to call "poor" all those who have particular needs, no matter how great. They are "needy," deserving of our immediate care, worthy of our special concern. We should indeed respond to them with our attention, our love, our ministry — but not under the rubric of responding to the poor.

The reason for restricting the definition of the poor to the economically poor should be quite obvious. To refer to all who have needs as being poor is to blur the very possibility of making an option for the poor. For if everyone is poor, how then can we make a preferential option?

I know that John Paul II, Mother Teresa, and the U.S. bishops Economic Pastoral (#173) have all at one time or another said that poverty can be described and defined in a variety of different ways. But the fact remains, in my opinion, that as soon as we broaden the definition beyond material deprivation and economic disadvantage, we water down the Christian's call to make the option for the poor. It is a fruitless and frustrating task to try to include everyone in the definition of the poor. Better to restrict the definition to a material sense, limiting it to those who suffer economic hardships. Then we can relate to others with different needs in their own right and not by straining to call them poor.

Another thing to clarify about the option for the poor is that the word "option" is more of a verb than a noun. I admit that this clarification may be grammatically questionable, but I believe it is politically correct. Let me explain with a comparison. When buying a new car, many "options" are available: air conditioning, stereo radio, radial tires, and so forth. But the option for the poor is not like that — just one of many options which I can pick and choose from in going about my Christian life. Rather it is a decisive action and a deliberate choice, reflecting values as well as desires, flowing from the core of my faith. The option for the poor is essential to my being a Christian, a follower of Jesus. As will become clear, this is one "option" that is not "optional"!

to be poor...is to be unemployed, to be on the margin of society...

But isn't the option for the poor a class option? Doesn't it divide society? To prefer one group in society over another group — in this instance, the poor over the non-poor — may seem to some to be contrary to the Christian's call to universal love. Indeed, this most probably accounts for the recent stress in Vatican documents on the use of the word "love" instead of "option" in describing the Christian's preferential stance toward the poor.

The first thing that must be acknowledged in response to this objection is that the option for the poor is a class option. But it does not create class, it simply recognizes its existence. In recognizing the existence of class, however, it also reinforces that reality. For it does imply "taking sides" in a situation of conflict — the real, everyday conflict that occurs between the poor and those who are not poor. The Christian cannot help but take sides.

That there are divisions in society is an historical fact. There have always been divisions based on race, sex, ethnic background, religion, geography, socio-economic status. The division between those who are poor and those who are not poor is fundamental — but it is not natural, i.e., inevitable. Social analysis reveals the root causes of that class division: the structures of inequitable power and unfettered profit referred to by John Paul II in The Social Concern of the Church (#37).

Social analysis also shows the conflicting consequences of that division: Housing patterns, educational levels, business opportunities, employment expectations, religious practices, cultural celebrations, political power, and so forth. The preferential option for the poor acknowledges the

...to be unable to deal with problems of daily existence...

causes and the conflicts. But the very "taking of sides" in the conflict is itself a challenge to work to transform society toward greater justice, thereby healing the divisions not through false harmony but by true structural change.

The option for the poor, then, is by no means meant to entail a hatred or rejection of the non-poor, or a promotion of violent class conflict. This is frequently an expressed fear of those who are wary of this option in our church today. Both John Paul II and Cardinal Ratzinger have cautioned against any Marxist class hatred being promoted by this option. But class hatred and rejection of the non-poor is hardly a demonstration of the solidarity with the poor based on the Christian commandment of love. Nor is making an option for the poor a rejection of any concern or ministry to the non-poor. That is why the expression used is "the preferential but non-exclusive option" — no one is excluded from Christian concern. As stressed above in defining the poor, there are certainly persons who are not poor but who are very much in need of our loving service. We do not exclude or reject them,

even if we are called to make a preferential option to relate to the poor.

Another point is very important to stress here. Opting for the poor does not at all involve a "romanticization" of the poor. It is not some fancy way of putting the poor on a special, unique pedestal — as if all goodness, all truth, all beauty, all grace is to be found only with the poor. Anyone of us who has ever been poor or who has ever lived and worked with the poor is all too painfully aware of the fact that original sin is fairly well distributed across class lines! There are no grounds, theological or empirical, for the notion that it is not to be found among the poor. No one group has the corner on virtue — or vice. Romanticizing the poor helps neither the poor nor the larger society.

ELEMENTS

Well, then, what can we say positively about defining the option for the poor? I want to suggest that it can best be understood as an orientation in the life of the Christian which has at least the following five inter-related elements.

1. Perspective. To make an option for the poor is to try to see reality through a particular lens. We try to see what is going on through the eyes of the poor, to try to perceive a particular social situation from the point of view of the poor. The Latin Americans speak of this effort as seeing reality "desde los pobres," where the preposition desde is roughly translated as "from," "from the side of," "on the part of," or "with the view of."

I am a middle-class, white male (and an overly-educated Jesuit at that!). Since I am not economically disadvantaged, I do not, of course, see the world as the poor see it. But I can make an effort to appreciate the perspective from which the poor view political and economic decisions, public and private policies, personal and institutional attitudes, and individual and corporate events. The point to be emphasized here is not that the perspective of the poor is the only true one, nor even the most important one. But it is the one frequently ignored or neglected or relegated to a subordinate position when important judgments and decisions are made.

Making the option for the poor means asking questions from the perspective of the poor. As I read about a hurricane or an earthquake, do I wonder how this natural disaster has affected those who live in the worst housing and are most dependent on public services? When I learn of a tax increase or a social budget cut, do I think of the consequences for those families who are already struggling to make ends meet? When I read a report that the economy is turning around, do I ask whether it is turning around for the poor?

2. Entry point to life and work. I may live and work with those who are not poor. But if I make an option for the poor, I can strive to enter into my life and work situations from the side of the poor. That is, the poor are on my mind and in my heart. Whatever I do — raise a family or teach, work in a factory or in an office, serve in a restaurant or in a church ministry — I can carry the poor with me. This means that in whatever I do and wherever I go I should try to bring with me the views,

problems, concerns, desires, visions, hopes and gifts of the poor.

Sometime ago I met a woman who had worked with poor inner city families in a large housing project on the East Coast. After several years, she moved to the Midwest to take a job with a management consulting firm involved in real estate planning. She was a highly efficient and pleasant person, and naturally advanced up the ladder in her firm. But there was something strikingly "different" about her attitudes and style. A profound and continuing sensitivity to the poor showed itself in her judgments.

3. Tool of evaluation. The option for the poor provides me with a basic question to ask whenever I evaluate a particular situation, decision or policy. That question is: "What does this mean to the poor?" In planning a family event, examining church social proposals, reviewing items in a budget, making a decision on priorities, I need to ask: what is happening to the poor as a result of this action? This is certainly not the only question to be asked. But it is an essential question if I have made an option for the poor.

Let me suggest a parallel. The Environmental Protection Agency of the U.S. government requires that before any major project can be undertaken (e.g., new buildings, highway construction), an "environmental impact statement" must be prepared. This study has to estimate what consequences such a project will have on the surrounding ecology. I believe that the option for the poor demands a "poor impact statement." That is, one factor by which we should weigh the worth of any

The point to be emphasized here is not that the perspective of the poor is the only true one, nor even the most important one. But it is the one frequently ignored, or neglected, or relegated to a subordinate position when important judgments and decisions are made.

project, the wisdom of any decision, or the urgency of any undertaking is: what will be the impact on the poor?

This particular dimension of the option for the poor was strongly emphasized by the U.S. Catholic bishops in their Economic Pastoral. They noted that the quality of the national discussion about the future of our economy affects the poor most of all, the poor both in this country and throughout the world. The direction of the economy must therefore be evaluated in terms of its impact on the life and dignity of the poor:

> Decisions must be judged in light of what they do for the poor, what they do to the poor and what they enable the poor to do for themselves. The fundamental moral criterion for all economic decisions, policies and institutions is this: They must be at the service of all people, especially the poor (#1).

4. *Accompanying.* The option for the poor involves us in the struggles to accompany the poor, to cooperate with their efforts, to be in solidarity with them. Accompanying places us neither in the front, as their leaders, nor in the back, as their followers. It puts us along side, as their companions. This requires a lot of

listening, of patient waiting, of silent learning. To be in solidarity with the poor, we need to strive to make our own, their preoccupations and fears, their hopes and plans.

To be honest, accompanying is not an easy stance to take for many of us who are not poor. We are more accustomed to take the lead, to give the orders. Our education and experiences put us at a supposed advantage and we are frequently uncomfortable in a position of accompanying. We expect that our opinions and choices will be the most influential. It is a challenge to show our solidarity with the poor by being true companions with them in the struggle. Oscar Romero, the martyred Archbishop of San Salvador, provided a wonderful model of accompaniment with the poor in his later years. Although a strong leader, he adopted a style of listening to the poor and learning from them, serving as a companion in their struggle for justice.

5. *Advocacy.* The option for the poor brings with it a bias in reaching decisions or settling disputes. It really does mean "taking sides". For in a point of controversy there are usually two or more sides with varying degrees of merit. One may enter such a controversy with the desire of helping to settle it as an arbitrator or as an advocate. An arbitrator comes in with a neutral stance, listens equally to all

The option for the poor involves us in the struggle to accompany the poor, to cooperate with their efforts, to be in solidarity with them.

sides, weighs all arguments, and from the merits of the case, judges which side appears to be more correct and just. An advocate, however, enters the dispute not neutral, but biased, favoring from the start one side over the other.

In controversies involving differences between the poor and the non-poor, the preferential option means that the Christian is an advocate on the side of the poor. The Christian does not speak for the poor but with the poor. Entering a dispute with such a bias is proper and justifiable. We know that if the argument by the non-poor side is in fact more valid, it stands a very good chance of being heard more favorably and winning — simply because it also has the advantages of position, power, influence,

education, friends, professional assistance (lawyers, research), publicity. Indeed, even if their argument lacks validity, these same strengths are still available to the affluent and they are more likely to win. But these same strengths are, of course, almost completely lacking for poor people if left on their own — whether or not they have the best case. This means that without the support of advocates the poor stand little chance of winning, no matter how valid their position may be.

MYTHS

As a final point of clarification, I want to mention certain popular myths which need to be exploded if the practice of the option for the poor is to be effective.

The first one — in my experience at least — is almost always brought up as an objection to efforts to change society to better the situation of the poor. Someone will inevitably argue: "Didn't Jesus say: 'The poor you have always with you'?" (John 12:8). The answer to that, of course, is that Jesus was making an empirical observation, not a prediction. Neither was he announcing a political platform! He was hardly recommending that we work to structure society so as to assure that the poor would always be in our midst. On the contrary, he was making a severe judgment since the presence of the poor is seen as a sign that the covenantal relationships of justice are not being achieved (Deuteronomy 15). Jesus' hearers took his remarks not as an encouragement but as a rebuke.

A second myth portrays the poor as somehow more fortunate than the non-poor and therefore not deserving of so much worry and attention on the part of society. After all, the myth says, "The poor are really happier and freer than us!" I believe it is very important to make a distinction here. There is, to be sure, a humanizing poverty which makes us happy by freeing us up from so many of the debilitating addictions of a consumer society. It is true that the poor do seem able to enjoy the simplicities of life much more easily than the non-poor. But there is also the very real dehumanizing poverty which is the degradation of hunger and homelessness, of lack of medical care and education, of fear for future survival. This is a condition which makes no one happy!

Third, those who would downplay the extent and the degree of poverty in North America will frequently raise the myth, "Our poverty is really not as great as their poverty." "Their," of course, refers to the Third World. It is true that the poverty conditions of many parts of Asia, Africa and Latin America are indeed severe. But the poor in this country also suffer greatly — from hunger, homelessness, poor health, powerlessness. And their poverty is compounded by the fact that it is experienced in the midst of an affluent society. The inner city or rural child who cannot go to school because of lack of decent shoes also knows from television that a consumerist ethos drives the majority of people in North America to a conspicuous and wasteful lifestyle. The child may measure her or his self-worth against the lifestyle of the rich and famous. In North America, more than elsewhere, the poor are subject to a loss of dignity, a self-contempt, which can lead to self-destructive behavior.

A fourth myth seems to me to be operative when the structural dimensions of poverty are being discussed. This is what I would call, with all due respect, the "Mother Teresa" myth. This is expressed sometimes as a critique of social action on behalf of justice. According to this myth, what Christians should be about in dealing with the poor is meeting their immediate needs and not struggling to change the structures of society. Those who propound this myth are reluctant to raise the justice issues. I'm reminded of the remark made several years ago by the courageous bishop of northern Brazil, Dom Helder Camara: "When I feed the hungry, I'm proclaimed a saint. When I ask why they are hungry, I'm called a communist!" While it is certainly an essential priority for the Christian to feed the hungry, clothe the naked and shelter the homeless, it is equally essential to work for justice through the transformation of the social, economic and political structures which perpetuate these conditions.

REFLECTION

Definitions and clarifications have abounded in our discussion of the option for the poor. But I feel that these are necessary if we are to make any positive movement in opting for the poor. The fears and/or skepticism which seem to paralyze us when we try to respond, as Christians, to the challenge of poverty, can frequently be traced to lack of clarity in what we're talking about. Understanding who the poor are and what the option is can seem very mundane. But without clear understanding, there is frustration at best, defeat at worst. The preferential option for the poor is too important to be stifled by either.

Of course, understanding also requires experience. We have to accompany the poor in some concrete way in order to escape from fruitless arguments and distracting myths. There is a reflection/action dynamic present here. Just as I need to think clearly in order to act effectively, so do I need to act concretely in order to think cogently. Then the option for the poor is alive for me.

CHAPTER IV

"Go and sell what you have and give to the poor; you will then have treasure in heaven. After that, come and follow me!"

Grounding the Task

hy does a Christian make an option for the poor? Why should one make such an option? These questions go to the heart of our discussion about the meaning and practice of opting for the poor in today's world. We are looking for the grounds for orienting our life and our work toward a preferential concern for the economically disadvantaged.

I am not talking here about a legal obligation but a moral invitation. In speaking of this orientation, there is no new commandment which says, "Thou shalt opt for the poor." But there is the clear invitation of Jesus: "Go and sell what you have and give to the poor; you will then have treasure in heaven. After that, come and follow me!" (Mark 10: 21).

There is something intrinsic to the following of Jesus which brings Christians to make the option for the poor.

Another way of putting this, I believe, is to say that, for the Christian, the concern for the poor may be a political position but it is not an ideological stance. By that I mean that opting for the poor involves us in the struggle for justice — a political task — but that the struggle itself is a consequence of a religious commitment, the result of a faith stance.

There are several solid theological reasons which ground the Christian's option for the poor. The most important of these reasons are, of course, rooted in the scriptures.

WAY OF THE INCARNATION

The answer to the question, "Why does the Christian make an option for the poor?" is really very simple and straightforward: because Jesus has made an option for the poor. The preferential option for the poor is the way of the Incarnation.

Paul makes this point quite clearly in his beautiful Christological hymn in the Letter to the Philippians. He speaks of the kenosis or "emptying" of Jesus in his assuming of our full humanity:

> Though he was in the form of God, he did not deem equality with God something to be grasped at. Rather, he emptied himself and took the form of a slave, being born in human likeness (Philippians 2: 6-7).

This "emptying" was for our sake, that he might more fully identify with us humans so that we could identify with him. In the Second Letter to the Corinthians, Paul explains what this means in terms of Jesus' poverty:

> You are well acquainted with the favor shown you by Our Lord Jesus Christ: how for your sake he made

himself poor though he was rich, so that you might become rich by his poverty (2 Corinthians 8: 9).

It is obvious from the Gospels that the option for the poor as the way of the Incarnation had very concrete consequences in the life of Jesus. This is clear in his birth, life-style, ministry, death and resurrection.

Regarding Jesus' birth, I must be honest and admit that my own earlier, simpler piety about Christmas scenes complete with snow and barnyard animals has been profoundly shaken by reading contemporary scriptural studies! Yet it is still very evident from the writings of scholars like Raymond Brown, for instance, that the early Christian community wanted to communicate a very important message in the infancy narratives. This is the message that Jesus made an option for the poor in the manner of his birth. It was God's plan that when the Second Person of the Blessed Trinity entered into human history it would not be as a princely babe born in a palace, nor as the well-off child of a wealthy merchant. Rather, the long-expected Messiah appeared in very humble surroundings — a stable — and was first visited by shepherds — the poor social outcasts of the region.

In his personal lifestyle, Jesus continued to exercise an option for the poor. In sketching the scene of the Purification, Luke emphasizes that Mary and Joseph made the offering of the poor, "a pair of turtledoves or two young pigeons" (Luke 2:24; Leviticus 12:8). It is true that Jesus himself was not a destitute person, desperately poor. He did not live in constant want, hungry and homeless. Yet he was able to describe himself in the following fashion: "The foxes have lairs, the birds in the sky have nests, but the Son of Man has nowhere to lay his head" (Matthew 8: 20).

His identification with the poor was in terms of a lifestyle of simplicity and lack of possessions. His ability to challenge the rich and the greedy was strengthened by his own authentic poverty.

The ministry of Jesus was another place where he showed an option for the poor. He began his public preaching with the reminder that he was sent "to bring good news to the poor" (Luke 4:18). He directly reached out to the poor, taking special note of widows who gave their last few coins to the Temple and to beggars who cried out on the side of the road.

In his death, Jesus was likewise with the poor — crucified between two thieves and buried in a stranger's tomb.

But it is in his life today that the Risen Lord Jesus most clearly makes known his preference for being with the poor. In the parable of the Last Judgment, he specifically identifies himself with those who are hungry, thirsty, naked, homeless, sick and imprisoned. These are the "least of my sisters and brothers" (Matthew 25: 40). To touch them is to touch Jesus. The mystery of the resurrection somehow involves this identification with the poor.

ORIENTATION OF THE GOSPEL

Another way of looking at the theological foundation for making the option for the poor is to note how much the whole spirit of scripture points to this option as central to the practice of faith. This is beautifully brought out in the Economic Pastoral, where the bishops discuss the Covenant's consequences in the life of Israel, and the consequences of the Reign of God for the disciples of Jesus (#35-52).

The Jewish scriptures repeatedly show God's concern for the poor and weak. This stance is primary (Psalm 103:6). But as a result of God's stance, there is also the demand that the poor be especially respected by the people of the Covenant. The God of Israel is always on the side of the poor, so must be the People of God. "Injure not the poor because they are poor, Nor crush the needy at the gate; For the Lord will defend their cause, And will plunder the lives of those who plunder them" (Proverbs 22: 22-23).

In the joyful hymn which Mary sings to celebrate the Incarnation, she reminds us of God's continuing special favor to the poor and oppressed:

God has shown might with the arm; God has confused the proud in their inmost thoughts. God has deposed the mighty from their thrones and raised the lowly to high places. The hungry God has given every good thing, while the rich God has sent empty away. (Luke 1: 51-53).

This special favor shows up frequently in the teaching of Jesus. Jesus called the poor "blessed" and promised that they would possess the Reign of God (Matthew 5:3; Luke 6:20). His "blessings" become more evident by contrast with the "woes" bestowed upon the rich (Luke 6: 24). Indeed, the Gospels are filled with strong warnings against riches. It is important to appreciate that the "woes" to the rich are fairly common, not because Jesus is against material possessions, but because he is against the attitudes and actions that frequently accompany the amassing of great possessions. These are the attitudes of greed, narrowness, insensitivity to the needy, self-sufficiency, pride and arrogance, etc. Moreover, in a structural sense, great wealth has direct and indirect relationships to great poverty. Woe to the rich who live in a society where there are poor!

Recall the parable of Dives and Lazarus, the rich man and the poor beggar at his door (Luke 16: 19-31). Dives is condemned not for being rich but for being blind to the needs of Lazarus, one so close to him. The parable about the foolish man who enlarges his granaries with no thought of enlarging his soul conveys the same message about the dangers of wealth (Luke 12: 16-21). One of Jesus' best known and most disturbing sayings is: "It is easier for a camel to pass through the eye of a needle than for a rich person to enter the kingdom of God" (Matthew 19: 24). How many tortured explanations have been made over the years to water down the force of this remark! One need not take "camels" and "needles" literally to sense the power of Jesus' challenge to the rich.

Two other elements of scriptural teaching seem to me to have relevance for grounding our option for the poor. The first is Jesus' mandate for simplicity in our apostolic missions. In sending out his disciples, Jesus gave them advice on how to be effective preachers: "Take nothing for the journey, neither walking staff nor travelling bag; no bread, no money. No one is to have two coats. Stay at whatever house you enter and proceed from there" (Luke 9: 3-4).

The message is direct: travel lightly, travel effectively. But the indirect message is no less important: travel lightly, travel close to the poor.

The second is found in the sharing and solidarity practiced in the early church (Acts 2:44-45; and 4:32-35). This distinguished the community and accounted for the respect it was accorded and the growth it experienced. Similarly, Paul urges the various communities to contribute to the poor in the church of Jerusalem. In doing so, they would be following Jesus' example of sharing himself (2 Corinthians 8 and 9).

FOCUS OF EVANGELIZATION

The option for the poor is a requirement of the Gospel. And the poor are a special focus of the preaching of that Gospel. This is evident in the ministry of Jesus. When he begins his task of proclaiming the Reign of God, Jesus specifically picks a text from Isaiah to lay out the elements of his mission. The first of these elements is: "to bring good news to the poor" (Luke 4: 18). Similarly, one of the signs which Jesus points to in order to reassure the disciples of John the Baptist of the authenticity of his mission is the fact that through his ministry the poor are being evangelized (Luke 7: 22).

Why are the poor a special focus of the preaching of the Gospel? To answer this, I believe it is helpful to recall what the Synod of Bishops said in Rome in 1971 in their ground-breaking statement, Justice in the World. Reviewing the signs of the times, including the great injustices of the contemporary world, the bishops spoke of the centrality of justice concerns to the church's task of evangelization:

Action on behalf of justice and participation in the transformation of the world fully appear to us as a constitutive dimension of the preaching of the Gospel, or, in other words, of the Church's mission for the redemption of the human race and its liberation from every oppressive situation (#6).

This connection between evangelization and justice was subsequently reinforced by Paul VI in his 1975 letter, Evangelization in the Modern World. According to the Pope, "Between evangelization and human advancement — development and liberation — there are in fact profound links" (#31).

Evangelization requires the struggle against injustice. But in a particular way, it is the poor who bear the burdens of injustice most heavily. It is not true, of course, that only the poor suffer injustice. But when injustice is experienced, those who are poor experience it most heavily. Blacks in the United States are unjustly treated, but poor Blacks feel this mistreatment most strongly. Women are discriminated against, but poor women face the worst consequences of sexism. If you are handicapped in today's society, you may experience injustice; but if you are both handicapped and poor, you feel all the more the social injustice.

What I am saying is that the poor face the concentration of injustice, the heaviest burdens of being victims of unjust attitudes and structures. For that reason, the struggle to bring about justice — a struggle central to the mission of evangelization — must pay special attention to the poor. The option for the poor becomes a test of authentic Gospel proclamation.

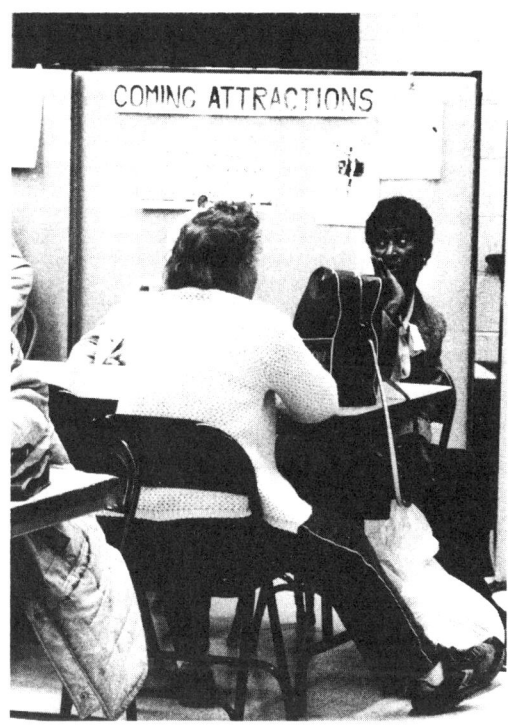

Poor women face the worst consequences of sexism.

EVANGELIZATION OF THE CHURCH

As I've just noted, it is the mission of the church to evangelize the poor. But the flip side of that is also true: the poor evangelize the church. In a mysterious but nonetheless very real way, the poor bring to the church at large the deepest meaning, the most profound implications of the Gospel. That this is so should not be surprising. For it is with the poor of the earth that Jesus has identified himself

(Matthew 25). By drawing close to the poor, we draw close to Jesus.

The Puebla statement from the Latin American bishops emphasized beautifully this point about the evangelizing potential of the poor.

> ...the poor challenge the Church constantly, summoning it to conversion; and many of the poor incarnate in their lives the evangelical values of solidarity, service, simplicity, and openness to accepting the gift of God (#1146).

The power of the poor to evangelize the church can perhaps best be seen when we look at history. There have certainly been periods when the church in its institutions, leadership and ministry has been alien to the poor and identified with the rich. One thinks of the princely courts of the Renaissance papacy or of the bishops who reinforced Latin American authoritarian dictatorships. But these times and places have been precisely the moments of doctrinal division, spiritual sterility and moral decadence. To pull away from the poor is to pull away from Jesus. And pulling away from Jesus definitely has consequences for the church of Jesus!

Great historical moments of reform within the church have always been marked by calls to draw closer to the poor. One thinks of Francis of Assisi challenging the medieval church, or Dorothy Day and Oscar Romero enlivening the contemporary church.

Why does this occur, this evangelization of the church by the poor? Georgetown University theology professor, Monika Hellwig, has asked the question, "Do the poor have privileged access to the meaning of the Gospel?" Is there some way or ways in which we can say — without romanticizing the poor — that the poor understand the Good News better than those who are not poor? According to Hellwig, there are a series of characteristic responses and attitudes which are often expressed by the poor and which do in fact open them up profoundly to the message of the Gospel:

(a) The poor know that they are in urgent need of redemption.

(b) The poor know not only their dependence on God and on powerful people but also their interdependence with one another.

(c) The poor rest their security not on things but on people.

(d) The poor have no exaggerated sense of their own importance.

(e) The poor expect little from competition and much from cooperation.

(f) The poor have no exaggerated need of privacy.

(g) The poor can distinguish between necessities and luxuries.

(h) The poor can wait because they have acquired a kind of dogged patience born of acknowledged dependence.

(i) When the poor are exposed to the Gospel, they interpret it very concretely and readily see it as having historical, practical import.

(j) When the poor have the Gospel preached to them, it sounds like good news and not like a threat or scolding.

(k) The promise of future salvation is truly present joy and therefore present incipient salvation to the poor.

(l) The really (desperately) poor can respond to the call of the Gospel with a certain abandonment and uncomplicated totality because they have so little to lose and are ready for anything.

(m) The fears of the poor are more realistic and less exaggerated because they already know that one can survive very great suffering and want. (*Tracing the Spirit*, James Hug, SJ, ed., Paulist Press, NY p. 145)

Reading over this list, I know that it is by no means a universal view of the poor. As I emphasized earlier, no "romantic" vision of the exclusive virtue of the poor should be promoted. Nevertheless, there is still a certain authentic ring to the list. This says to me, yes, the condition of the poor woman and poor man can in fact open them up in uniquely sensitive ways to the values of the Gospel. And without the close association with the poor and with their struggles — an association made possible through the practice of opting for the poor — the rest of the church is deficiently evangelized.

SOLIDARITY WITH JESUS

The last point which I feel touches on the theological foundation for the option for the poor relates to the spirituality of being poor with the poor Jesus.

There is an important thread in the history of spirituality which has emphasized the great value of being poor — not just spiritually poor, poor in spirit, but actually poor, poor in reality. Obviously, I am not speaking of a material deprivation which degrades the human spirit. Rather, I'm referring to an absence of material possessions, which enables one to be unencumbered, free, open to God's gifts in a new and surprising fashion.

One example of a spiritual tradition which calls for an identification with the poor in the search for an identification with Jesus is found in the Spiritual Exercises of Saint Ignatius of Loyola. There is a dynamic in the Exercises whereby at each critical moment of making a choice to follow Jesus, we are asked to pray for "the highest spiritual poverty, and, if it be God's will, even actual poverty." This prayer is made in the key meditations suggested by Ignatius, treating the call of Christ the King and the various responses — of greater and lesser generosity — which can be made to this call.

But it is important to note that according to this Ignatian dynamic one doesn't choose poverty for itself. This would be an ascetical choice. Such a choice might have some validity, but it is not what is associated with the preferential option for the poor. Rather one makes an apostolic choice, a choice of mission. One chooses to be in solidarity with Christ, who is poor, who is with the poor and who is bringing justice to the poor. The option for the poor, then, becomes a necessity for those who want to be with Jesus in the work of the Reign of God.

REFLECTION

I emphasized at the start of this chapter that the option for the poor, while involving a political component of engagement in the struggle to transform society toward justice, is primarily a religious commitment. The centrality of that commitment to the living out of the Christian faith is seen in its being the commitment of Jesus. Making the preferential option for the poor is essential to the following of Jesus, to incorpo-

The message is direct: travel lightly, travel close to the poor.

rating the teaching of scripture into our lives and work, to evangelizing and being evangelized.

The future of our church in North America — and worldwide — is, I firmly believe, dependent on the authenticity of our option for the poor. In the struggle to live out that option is our surest contact with the poor.

We must be imaginative and creative enough to find multiple ways to serve the poor and bring about the transformation of society.

Applying the Option

But what do we do? That question comes up finally and persistently, after all the clarifications and definitions, scripture and theology. How do we go about putting the option for the poor into practice, applying it in the concrete situations of our North American context?

Several years ago, I heard Cardinal Paulo Evaristo Arns of San Paulo, Brazil, speak on the theme of the preferential option for the poor. He described how practicing the option meant that the church would suffer persecution but would also undergo profound transformation toward greater Gospel fidelity. He added, however, that to opt for the poor in Latin America was not that difficult. Since the overwhelming majority of Latin Americans are in fact poor, to opt for the poor simply means to opt for the people!

In North America, on the other hand, it is not so simple. Though there are many of our citizens living in poverty, the majority of people are not in fact poor. How do we effectively engage in the societal transformation which is central to the option? Are there many ways to go about this task?

Addressing these questions can move us effectively to action in solidarity with the poor. We need to be creative in seeking responses which can involve all Christians, not just a few.

MANY WAYS

I believe that there are two points which need to be stressed very strongly, right at the outset of our discussion about applying the option for the poor. First, avoid reductionism; second, emphasize structuralism.

There is a great problem with talking about the option for the poor in a univocal fashion, of understanding it in a very narrow way. I have heard many discussions in which opting for the poor is reduced to work which can only be done by those with direct, immediate, hands-on, continuous and full-time contact with the poor. Those who work in soup kitchens, teach in inner-city schools, go to the Third World missions and so forth are seen to be the only true practitioners of the option for the poor. The problem with this sort of reductionism is clear: it excludes everyone who is not thus directly involved with the poor — and that means the majority of Christians! The option for the poor then becomes the exclusive virtue of a privileged few rather than the demanding vocation of all.

Moreover, the option for the poor should always be seen as part of the wider transformation of the structures of society which keep the poor, poor. As I have emphasized before, the fact that there are poor in North America and in other parts of the world is not an accident. It is the explicit outcome, the necessary result, of the way we have structured our society politically, economically and culturally. Inequitable concentration of wealth, income and power lead to tax laws, employment policies, welfare programs, housing plans and other policies and structures which directly and adversely affect the poor. Therefore the option for the poor will never be satisfied with responses only of charity. There must also be a commitment to justice, to structural change.

What I am suggesting is that the ways of practicing the option for the poor should be multiple. We need to be creative and inventive if we are to be authentic and effective.

Several years ago I read of a set of distinctions about the meaning of the option for the poor which a group of Jesuits involved in Third World ministries had devised. I found the distinctions very helpful and suggestive of further ways to approach the topic as individuals, families, communities and institutions. Let me offer here a framework, inspired in part by that original effort, to clarify the variety of ways in which the option for the poor can be practiced.

OPTIONS FOR THE POOR

   I. Negative

  II. Positive

      A. Affective

      B. Effective

         1. Direct

         2. Indirect

NEGATIVE OPTION

First, there is a negative option for the poor: we don't do things — specific actions, regular practices, style of life, etc. — which oppress the poor. I would suggest that simply by itself this would be quite an accomplishment! If in personal and corporate ways, we did not oppress the poor, major strides would be made toward transforming society.

This negative option has many practical consequences. For example, we do not patronize stores that discriminate against the poor through payment of low wages, racist or sexist practices, opposition to trade unions and so forth. Nor do we do business with banks that refuse loans to low-income neighborhoods ("red-lining"), or hold investments in South Africa. We refuse to purchase certain products — e.g., foods, clothes, appliances — that are the result of oppressive labor conditions in this country or in Third World countries. We raise our families and teach our children not to be wasteful of the goods of the earth, recognizing that, in an age of interdependence, what and how we use the world's resources really does affect the poor. Similarly, our business practices such as hiring and dealing with unions do not go against the interests of the poor.

One result of practicing this negative option can be involvement in a variety of boycotts. This isn't always easy. A friend of mine told me that what she eats these days seems to depend as much on ideology as on taste! We can get greatly frustrated worrying about whether grapes can or cannot be eaten this season, whether or not a particular brand of electric bulbs gives off just and peaceful light, or whether we should patronize this store or that store.

Viewed from the perspective of practicing the option for the poor, however, boycotts become a very simple and direct way of being on the side of the poor and also educating ourselves and others about the structures of poverty. Involvement in a boycott means recognition of economic power and the interconnectedness – structural relationships – among those who hold power. To have a negative stance toward cooperating with, participating in, institutions, structures, buisnesses, markets, etc., which oppress the poor is part and parcel of the option for the poor.

But can we ever really be completely "pure" in our current capitalistic economic system here in North America? There are so many hidden ways in which we can get entangled in unjust structures–products we buy, restaurants we eat in, banks that process our accounts, etc. True. But there are still enough choices which we can make, personally and corporately, to try to affect social justice for the poor. We need to take the steps we can and not use the complexity of the situation as an excuse. We have to avoid the paralysis of moralism and legalism. With creativity and good will, Interfaith Committee on Corporate Responsibility in New York and Center for New Creation in Virginia, for example, offer help in choosing socially responsible investments for groups as well as for individuals.

AFFECTIVE OPTION

The option for the poor also has a *positive* dimension. I would begin by emphasizing the positive *affective* aspect. Opting for the poor means loving the poor, letting the poor touch my heart, move my

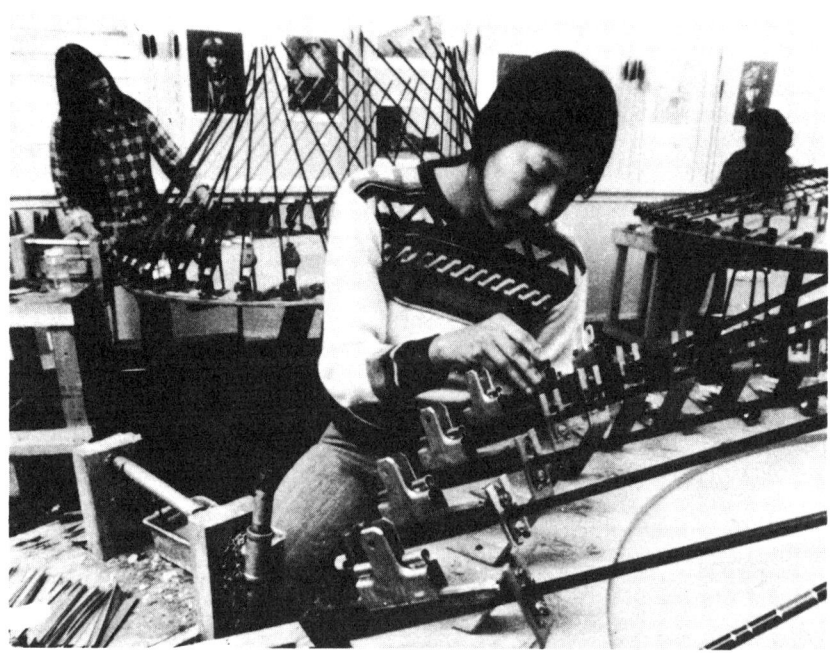

Socially responsible investments encourage employment and independence.

emotions. I'm not speaking of a romantic affectivity that glamorizes the poor. That usually doesn't translate well into political action, into structural change. Rather, I refer to the very basic emotions of reaction to the situation of the poor, to the sufferings of the people. Compassion, sorrow, anger, fear, frustration, sadness — these and many more feelings reveal the quality and character of my option for the poor.

What happens to me when I see a homeless person begging on the street or sleeping in a doorway? What moves within me when I hear about a fire in a crowded slum tenement that kills an entire family? How do I react when I read of a budget cut that removes young single mothers from food stamp benefits? What do I feel when I see on television the thousands who are starving in African refugee camps? Reflections arising from these and other similar questions help me evaluate my affective stance toward the poor.

Do the poor ever enter into my prayer? This is a key test of my practice of the option for the poor. Letting the situations of the poor, the persons of the poor, come into my prayer is a sign of the positive affective solidarity I have with the poor. Reading the scripture from the side of the poor — noting the consequences for the poor and oppressed of the words of the prophets about justice or the parables of Jesus about the Reign of God — gives an entirely different perspective to God's revelation. It was precisely such a reading of scripture which gave rise to Liberation Theology in Latin America and the growth of the preferential option for the poor.

But to have this affective option for the poor, to really love the poor, requires first and foremost that we personalize our experience with the poor, give them names and faces. We must stop talking about the poor, about "them," and speak of John and Maria, individuals that we know personally. To opt for the poor means to make friends with the poor. The poor cannot remain merely nameless statistics or faceless trends. They are persons whom I get to know and to love — they touch my heart.

DIRECT EFFECTIVE OPTION

In speaking of a positive effective option for the poor, there is first of all the direct effective option. This is the privileged opportunity of those who live and work immediately with the poor. It takes a variety of forms: community organizing in a poor inner city neighborhood or a Third World barrio, serving in a soup kitchen or shelter for the homeless, caring for the elderly poor in a nursing home, tutoring young children from poor families, working in a poor parish, teaching in an inner city school, providing health care for migrant workers, creating grassroots movements among rural poor in Third World countries, working in refugee camps, ministering to the forgotten poor in prisons, defending the indigents in court and so forth.

The common note of this direct effective option for the poor is that it engages us in an immediate, hands-on involvement with the poor, involvement in

their lives, their struggles, their despairs and their hopes. It is usually a full-time, full-scale, full-resource involvement. It is frequently accompanied by living with the poor, sharing their daily bread on a regular basis. Whether exercising charity or promoting justice, this option has explicit and visible consequences. The hungry are fed, the homeless are sheltered, the illiterate are taught.

Obviously, not all work which is a direct effective option for the poor will be successful or satisfying. The poor may treat you obnoxiously and ungratefully. But the option is nevertheless a direct experience of the reality of the lives of specific poor persons. As such, it is a privileged contact with Jesus.

INDIRECT EFFECTIVE OPTION

I feel it is also critically important to recognize an indirect effective option for the poor. While lacking an immediate, hands-on characteristic, this style of opting for the poor is nonetheless effective in touching the structures and attitudes which perpetuate poverty. The preferential option for the poor comes alive in the effort to live and work in ways which transform society toward greater justice for all, especially for the poor.

Advocacy, for example, is key to attacking poverty and the oppression of the poor. In Washington, DC, a group like NETWORK lobbies Congress for more adequate and just welfare reform, while Bread for the World works to counter military aid to Third World countries. Research is also a necessary component in fighting against poverty. The Center of Concern, for example, studies the global debt problem in order to show the impact on the poor of the policies of the international banks and to suggest alternative approaches to addressing the issue. Education is a third way of practicing an indirect effective option for the poor. Efforts are made by many individuals and groups to make more widely known the situation of poverty in this county and around the world, with a view to eliciting both charitable response for the needy and political action for change.

Indirect effective option for the poor means that all that we do, whatever we do, is done in such a way that we are contributing — personally and corporately — to the transformation of society so that the poor are not suffering, not oppressed. Parents raising a non-poor family can be in solidarity with the poor through the values of respect and justice which they communicate to their children. A parish in a suburban area may not have any poor in its immediate congregation. But what goes on in the life of the parish? What is preached about in the sermons, taught in the school, celebrated in the liturgy, practiced in the budget, etc.? A retreat house may open its doors occasionally to poor persons who cannot pay the fees. But what goes on in the regular retreats which cater mainly to non-poor? What sort of spirituality is encouraged? Is the Jesus of the Gospels — the Jesus who was poor and was with the poor — fully introduced to retreatants?

Many persons who are active in the educational apostolate wonder, worry, about their relationship to the preferential option for the poor. Is it possible to exercise an option for the poor in the typical middle class Catholic school? I've thought a lot about that question, particularly since the Jesuit Order to which I belong is so deeply involved in education. To be honest, very few poor students enroll in Jesuit schools — the tuition and life-style are simply too expensive. If the only way to practice an option for the poor, in

To really love the poor...requires that we personalize our experience with the poor.

education circles, is reduced to directly teaching the poor, then the typical Catholic school is certainly unable to opt for the poor.

But if this option is seen in much wider terms, then there definitely is a possibility. The way we teach, the material we bring in, the values we promote, the questions we raise, the directions we point to, the persons and situations we expose students to: all this and much more provide an opportunity to be in solidarity with the poor. The test, of course, is the end product of the education. What is the effect on the students who have gone to this particular school, on the life-style they lead, the votes they cast, the professional vocations they choose, the business policies they practice, the language they use, the stance they take toward societal change, the way they raise their families?

This is an empirical question: are the students who have passed through St. X High School or University of St. Y known for their commitment to justice and peace, to changing society so that the poor are not oppressed? If so, then the faculty and administrators of those schools did indeed practice the option for the poor — even if they did not teach poor students directly. Of course, it is important for a school to raise scholarship funds and increase its enrollment of the poor. But in itself, that is not sufficient for the school to be considered as opting for the poor. Its fundamental educational orientation must be touched.

This indirect approach to the option for the poor has wide implications for many other institutions besides schools. Hospitals, for example, practice an option for the poor by offering free treatment to poor patients.

This is certainly essential and widely practiced in many church-related healthcare institutions. But these institutions must also examine their employee practices, investment portfolios, purchasing policies, and corporate political stances. Items such as these also affect the poor — indirectly but very significantly.

I must admit that I make this point about the indirect effective option for the poor with much vigor for reasons that are both political and personal.

Politically, I feel that unless the indirect effective option is lifted up as a valid and authentic exercise, there is the possibility of significantly narrowing effective action for and with the poor. If opting for the poor is reduced only to direct engagement, we risk the twin dangers of either *(1)* letting ourselves and others have an excuse for not being involved ("I can never live among the poor") or *(2)* making it only an exercise in charity and not in the transformation of justice ("forget the politics of change, just serve the poor").

Personally, I've spent most of my professional time and energy doing research, advocacy and education which does not involve much direct contact with the poor. So I have to ask myself bluntly: can I be said to practice an option for the poor? The answer is no, if a simple reductionist understanding prevails. But if my research, advocacy and education is done on behalf of the poor, aimed at effecting the structural changes in society which are necessary to improve the situation of the poor, then I have exercised an option for the poor.

Having said that, I will still emphasize that the indirect effective option for the poor does require some direct contact with poor persons. I will return to this point in the next chapter.

REFLECTION

In addressing the application of the preferential option, how worthwhile is it to make all these distinctions? Is it simply an abstract intellectual exercise, ultimately distracting us from the basic thrust of the option for the poor? I don't think so.

The reason I have presented this detailed framework of response for putting the preferential option for the poor into practice, is that I firmly believe it is an option which is central to the Christian life, to the following of Christ. Therefore it must be open to every Christian, not narrowed to only an elite few. We must be wide enough in our imagination and creative enough in our action to find multiple ways to serve the poor and bring about the transformation of society by being on the side of the poor.

CHAPTER VI

*The transformation of social structures
begins with and is always accompanied
by a conversion of heart.*

Affecting
Our Lives

U ltimately, if the preferential option for the poor is to come alive in North America, it has to be fully integrated into our personal lives. We have to respond as persons. That means not simply as persons individually, but as persons in community.

The problem of poverty and the suffering of the poor — our sisters and brothers — is, as I have stressed repeatedly throughout this book, a structural problem. It is a matter of how we have structured our society through the economic, political and cultural institutions in which we live our lives. In order to achieve justice for the poor, structural transformation is an absolute necessity. Economics as if people mattered, the politics of participation, a culture which respects everyone: these are societal goals which have particular significance for the poor.

Structural transformation, of course, requires personal transformation also. It is not a question of "either/or" but "both/and." The U.S. bishops put this very well in the closing section of the Economic Pastoral:

> The transformation of social structures begins with and is always accompanied by a conversion of the heart. As disciples of Christ each of us is called to a deep personal conversion and to "action on behalf of justice and participation in the transformation of the world." By faith and baptism we are fashioned into a "new creature"; we are filled with the Holy Spirit and a new love that compels us to seek out a new profound relationship with God, with the human family and with all created things. . . .But personal conversion is not gained once and for all. It is a process that goes on through our entire life. Conversion, moreover, takes place in the context of a larger faith community: through baptism into the church, through common prayer and through our activity with others on behalf of justice (#328).

The personal implications of the option for the poor for us here in North America call for considerable prayer and struggle, creativity and humility. I want to touch on three key points: accepting my own weakness, simplifying my life style and being with the poor.

WEAKNESS

How poor am I? What is my personal experience of poverty? In dealing with that question, I'm going to emphasize something here which may at first glance seem to contradict an important point I made earlier. I have stressed that it is not helpful to speak of a variety of different kinds of poverty — "spiritual" poverty "psychological" poverty, and so forth. We should keep the definition of the poor very simple and very clear: the economically disadvantaged, the materially deprived, who as a consequence suffer powerlessness, exploitation and oppression.

"...that there are poor in North America and other parts of the world is not an accident. It is the expected outcome...of the way we have structured our society, politically, economically and culturally. Each of us is called to a deep personal conversion and to action on behalf of justice..."

But there is, nevertheless, a recognition of my own personal weakness as an analogous experience of poverty. And this recognition is central to the personal implications of practicing the option for the poor. I am not poor, never have been and probably never will be. But there are things that I do experience about myself that can give me clues at least of what it means to be poor. I need to reflect seriously on these experiences. There is a kind of window on the experience of the poor in my experience of the existential limits of my creaturehood, of the lonely moments of my humanity, of the lack of freedom arising from my middle class viewpoints and fears of change, of the cultural constraints of militarism, of the political frustrations of being unable to effect desired change, of the personal tendencies to selfishness and sin.

Let me share a story of a personal experience which has helped me to reflect on the limitations experienced by the poor. Shortly after joining the Center of Concern, I went to study Spanish for the first time in Cuernavaca, Mexico. Struggling with the newness of the language and the strangeness of the culture gave me many occasions to feel very weak and vulnerable. But one incident in particular made me experience something of the weakness and powerlessness so common to the poor. I was living with a large family while attending the language institute — a wonderful way to practice my Spanish, since the family spoke no English. It was a household of very simple means which supplemented its income by taking in students. The father of the family had been ill and usually did not eat meals with us. One evening, he suffered a heart attack and became unconscious. Without a phone, without ordinary transportation, the family struggled to get the father to the local hospital. I was enlisted to help, both physically and spiritually. By the time we reached the hospital, the father had died.

When I tried to speak some words of comfort to the mother and children, all my newly-learned Spanish — meager as it was — completely left me. Vocabulary, grammar and pronunciation evaporated. I was reduced to the basic body language of lots of hugs and holding of hands. I felt very, very weak and powerless. I wanted so much to share my sorrow with them, to offer some words of consolation, to lead a simple prayer. By nature and training, I am a verbal, articulate person. But at that critical moment, I was speechless.

I've often recalled that incident in reflecting on the feeling of frustration which must be the daily lot of the poor in this country and around the globe: wanting to do something but being unable to, experiencing a profound weakness in the face of so many desires. My experience of weakness was certainly very minor, even trivial, in comparison with the powerlessness of the poor. But it has helped me to appreciate at least a little the situation of the poor. And it has convinced me that one of the personal implications of opting for the poor is the effort to get in touch with our own weaknesses and vulnerabilities, that we might become that much more sensitive to the lot of the poor.

SIMPLICITY

We live on a globe marked by profound interconnections. Sometimes this is described as "interdependence" — stressing particularly the economic connections between rich and poor countries. But

> To opt for the poor means to opt for a more simple and consequently less oppressive lifestyle.

"interdependence" can be a deceptive word, seeming to imply a certain equality between the parties involved in mutual dependence. Because of the power and money of the rich countries of the North, however, there really is no equal status in their relationships with the poor nations of the South. Investments, trade, aid, financial arrangements, military presence and cultural influences all set up patterns more favorable to the rich than to the poor. In a world of scarce resources, affluence creates poverty.

A friend of mine from the Third World helped me see this in structural terms. She told me several years ago: "Interdependence? That just means that you enter and we depend!" Without a power analysis, the term masks a situation in which those of us who live in the so-called "developed" world profit greatly from the deplorable situation in the "developing" world.

What are the personal implications of this global situation when we come to make the preferential option for the poor? We need to recognize the interrelationships between affluent consumption patterns and the suffering of the poor. Recognizing that, we need to make an effort to simplify our life styles. As the popular expression puts it: "live simply, so that others may simply live."

There is no direct, "one-to-one" relationship, for example, between curtailing food waste in a U.S. college cafeteria and providing basic food necessities to a refugee camp in the Sudan. But the overall structural connections between affluence and poverty — one creating the other — are very real. So to opt for the poor means also to opt for a more simple and, consequently, less oppressive life style.

Simplicity of life style — in food, dress, housing, travel, recreation, and so forth — is also a freeing experience. For it enables us to enter more effectively into a struggle to break free from the power of a consumer society. Consumerism traps us in a never-ending cycle of "more and more", a cycle subtly — and not so subtly! — reinforced by advertising and by the reigning cultural patterns. "Lifestyles of the Rich and Famous" is not only a popular television show in the United States. It is also a societal norm pushed by manufacturers and advertisers.

In a consumer society like the United States a dynamic develops which catches all of us almost unknowingly. Many years ago the eminent psychologist and social critic, Erich Fromm, described this situation. According to Fromm, the consumerist dynamic moves items from being superfluous, to convenient, to necessary, to indispensable. I began by really not needing this item — e.g., an electric toe nail clipper. But it does become handy to have around. And then I find that I really do need it. And then I discover that I can't leave home without it! The same item all the time — the blessed electric toe nail clipper — but the consumerist dynamic has trapped me!

Personally, I experience this consumerist dynamic each time I pack my bag for a trip. Something I could leave behind a few years ago, now must urgently be squeezed into my bag. That's not because I'm greedy and extravagant. Or at least that's not the primary reason! But I live in a society which constantly tells me that I won't be happy without more and more possessions to make me happy. And at some level I have come to accept that message.

Unfortunately, this consumerist dynamic has disastrous results for the poor of both the First and the Third Worlds. This is the consequence of the structures of our interdependent economy. It means that scarce resources are diverted for consumer goods, luxury items, while basic necessities go unmet. This is certainly contrary to a Christian pattern of living which manifests an option for the poor. The U.S. Bishops' Economic Pastoral has this in mind, I believe, when it speaks of the need to examine our lifestyles:

> At times we will be called upon to say no to the cultural manifestations that emphasize values and aims that are selfish, wasteful and opposed to the Scriptures. Together we must reflect on our personal and family decisions and curb unnecessary wants in order to meet the needs of others. There are many questions we must keep asking ourselves: Are we becoming ever more wasteful in a "throwaway" society? Are we able to distinguish between our true needs and those thrust on us by advertising and a society that values consumption more than saving? All of us could well ask ourselves whether as a Christian prophetic witness we are not

Together we must reflect on our personal and family decisions and curb unnecessary wants in order to meet the needs of others.

The poor become friends because of the time I have spent with them, learning about them, learning from them.

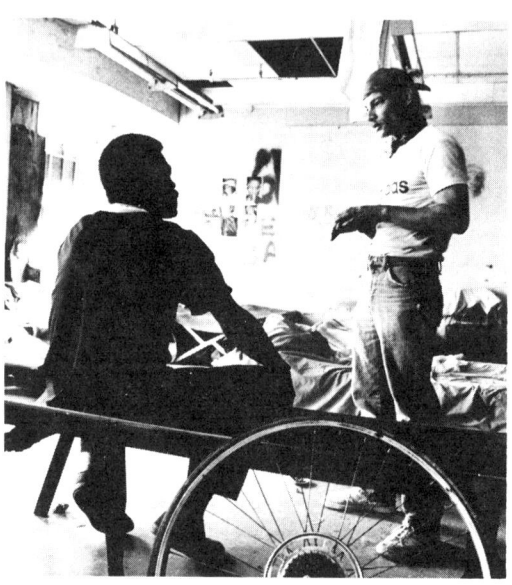

called to adopt a simpler lifestyle in the face of the excessive accumulation of material goods that characterizes an affluent society (#334).

Struggling to simplify our lifestyles because of our option for the poor affects us at every level. Our personal choices, our family and community decisions, our workplace styles: all are involved. We need an "examination of conscience" to help us ask simple questions about simple lifestyle. Church-related institutions should strive to be exemplary in this matter, to provide a counter-cultural witness of simplicity. This seems to be one implication of the option for the poor as mentioned in *The Social Concern of the Church* when John Paul II states that the church cannot ignore the needs of the poor in favor of "superfluous church ornaments and costly furnishings for divine worship." (#31)

The ability to make free choices for greater simplicity calls upon our creativity, for we need to imagine new and different ways of maintaining and enjoying ourselves. It also calls for a sense of humor. Nothing can be more deadly to the spirit than a simple lifestyle carried to serious extremes!

BEING WITH THE POOR

When I discussed the importance of the indirect effective option for the poor in the previous chapter, I indicated that not all of us are called to have immediate, full-time, hands-on experience with the poor. But now I want to add with great emphasis that those of us who lack this direct involvement must, if our option for the poor is to be lasting and authentic, have some direct experience with the poor. Such experience personalizes the poor. It enables us to stop talking about "the poor" and talk rather about "poor people," about "John and Maria." The poor become friends because of time I have spent with them, learning about them, learning from them.

Exercising an option for the poor means, therefore, that being with the poor is essential. Indeed, this direct being with the poor makes the various other ways of opting for the poor more real, more grounded and solid. I will want to be serious about the negative option for the poor because I will have seen what the poor suffer and I won't want to do anything that would hurt my friends. I will have a depth to my affective option for the poor because I have real persons in my heart, not just abstractions or statistics. And I will struggle to be authentic in my indirect effective option for the poor because I will have recognized in the lives of my friends the structural dimensions of poverty and the need to transform those structures toward greater justice.

But how do we go about "being with" the poor? This requires a creative approach to finding ways to spend time. So-called "insertion" or "explosive" or "urban plunge" experiences provide wonderful opportunities to be with the poor in a totally different setting for a time.

Is this using the poor? No, it's needing the poor — more than they need us, in fact. There is, of course, a danger that this personal implication of an option for the poor could result in utilizing poor people for my own growth, my own spiritual edification. This would be unfortunate and simply unacceptable. The only response I know to that danger is to be explicitly aware of it. And, as much as possible, to let the poor do the inviting. They will be quick to point out whether or not they are feeling used.

Several years ago, Father Pedro Arrupe, the superior general of the Jesuit Order, spoke of the need to practice a "tithing of time" for direct being with the poor. He remarked that, "Some Christians are called to spend all of their time with the poor, but all Christians are called to spend some of their time with the poor." Just as we are called to find ways to give a portion of our material resources to the needs of the poor, so we are called to find ways to share our time with the poor. Such "tithing" may involve an hour a week, a day a month, a week a year, or an extended period at some point in my life. It provides us with the opportunity to be with the poor, to be changed, to be changing.

One result of this being with the poor is that memory takes on a political function. By that I mean that the names and faces of the poor, of my friends, enter into the choices I make to transform society. This is the "subversive" memory which undermines the cultural constraints of the status quo. I believe that this is what Mahatma Gandhi was speaking about many years ago when he is said to have given advice like this to a follower:

Picture the poorest, most abject, oppressed and helpless human being you have ever met. Then ask yourself as you face any decision: will what I do now, the step I take now, have any consequences for the poor person's human dignity, rights, well being? As I focus my attention on this poor person while evaluating my decision, I will find all my doubts, anxieties, hesitancies, my very self, melting away.

REFLECTION

Making an option for the poor does have its personal implications. These implications are not all clearly defined and easily organized. But they certainly relate to how I come to grips with my own weakness, how I make choices regarding my lifestyle, and how I find time to be with persons who are poor. As opting for the poor becomes more a part of my life, of the life of the families, communities and organizations to which I belong, of the work and activities in which I engage, the personal implications will become more obvious.

"Me llamo Jesus! My name is Jesus!"

Conclusion

pting for the poor is central to our life as Christians. As North Americans, we have a special challenge. Poverty here is at once hidden and obvious, forgotten and blatant. Our culture wants to deny it. Our conscience can't ignore it.

To me, the challenge of opting for the poor takes names and faces. In the inner-city Washington neighborhood where I live in a small Jesuit community, Sam Stephen's daily visits to our door remind me of the loneliness of the elderly poor. Mrs. Charles' working hard to hold down two jobs with minimum pay in order to raise many children and grandchildren reveals to me the strengths of poor women. Michael, thirteen years old and struggling with reading lessons in the local school, teaches me about the problems the poor experience with education. The street people who walk by my window each morning at 6:00 A.M. leaving the night shelter to head to the soup kitchen for breakfast, tell me of our nation's lack of priority in meeting the basic needs of the poor. Harvey, who hangs out with the drug addicts on the corner one block away, shows me the hopelessness of poor Black teenagers in today's society. Ricardo, the young Salvadoran refugee who lives in our community, opens up to me the consequences for the poor of the U.S.'s destructive "national security" policies. These are the people with whom I am called to be in solidarity. For the deepest reasons of faith, opting for the poor means being on the side of the poor in a struggle for justice in our nation and in our world. For my faith tells me that there is where Jesus is, with the poor. Indeed, he is poor himself.

A graced experience I had several years ago revealed this truth to my head and to my heart.

I lived in Latin American for a year in the mid-1970s. Studying Spanish in Bolivia for a few months, I appreciated the fact that an easy way to improve a new language is to practice it with small children. They are all too eager to help, to correct, and to make fun of adults! One day I accompanied a Bolivian Jesuit to a residence outside Cochabamba where very poor orphans lived. As I walked through the crowd of youngsters who ran up to talk to me, one little guy in particular was trying to get my attention. He clearly was very poor, shabbily dressed and he had a bad limp. I soon realized that he also was retarded. Because I felt that he was not going to be of much help for my practice of Spanish, I moved away from him to seek out some other youngsters.

Slowly, the young boy turned and sought out the older Jesuit who was with me. The man picked him up and asked him "!Como te llamas, nino? What is your name, little boy?" I remember to this day what that little boy answered. "!Me llamo Jesus! My name is Jesus!"

I missed a chance to meet Jesus, because I turned aside from a very real opportunity of opting for the poor. For me, that's what this challenge of the option for the poor is all about. Do we allow ourselves to meet Jesus?

Justice and the Poor in Scripture

LIBERATION OF THE POOR AND OPPRESSED

Exodus 3:7-19 God delivers Israel
Leviticus 19:9-15 Sharing goods of earth
Leviticus 25:1-19-;35-38 The Sabbatical Year
Deuteronomy 10:16-19 Justice for the orphan and widow
Deuteronomy 24:17-22 Remember, and pass on justice to others
Deuteronomy 30:15-20 Choose life
Job 24:2-14 Evil of injustice
Psalms: 34,69,72, 82,107,146 Justice for the poor
Psalms: 2,72,47,93,110 Kingdom psalm good news
Jeremiah 7:1-11 Do not oppress
Jeremiah 21:3-7;13-17 Rescue the weak
Amos 2:6-7 Crushing the poor
Amos 5:21-24 Let justice flow
Amos 6:1-6 Woe to those who worry about comfort
Amos 8:4-7 Against exploiters

Micah 2:1-2 Against the rich
Micah 3:1-4 Against rulers who oppress
Micah 4:1-7 The peace that will come
Micah 6:9-13 Violence of the rich
Habbakuk 2:5-17 Curses on oppressors
Zechariah 8:14-17 Doing justice

THE REIGN OF GOD AND THE POOR

Matthew 5:3-11 The Beatitudes
Matthew 5:20-38 New standards of justice and love
Matthew 6:24 God and money
Matthew 11:2-5 Jesus' identity in service
Matthew 19:11-24 The rich man and the Reign
Matthew 25:31-40 The Reign is yours
Mark 10:17-31 Riches and renunciation
Mark 10:42-45 The use of power
Mark 12:41-44 The widow's offering
Luke 1:46-45 The greatness of God shown forth
Luke 4:16-21   Jesus' mission
Luke 6:20-26   The Beatitudes
Luke 7:18-23   Jesus' identity
Luke 10:25-37   The Good Samaritan
Luke 12:15-21   The rich fool
Luke 14:15-24   The invited guests
Luke 15:11-32   The experience of salvation
Luke 16:16   Reversal of values
Luke 16:19-31   The rich man and Lazarus
Luke 18:18-30   Danger of riches
Luke 19:1-10   Zaccheus
John 6:25-59   Work for eternal life
John 13:1-17   Jesus washes his disciples' feet
John 13:34-35   Discipleship

Acts 2:44-47 Sharing goods
Acts 4:32-35 Holding all in common
1 Corinthians 15:24-28 All under the rule of Jesus
2 Corinthians 8:9-15 Jesus became poor
Philippians 2:5-11 Jesus emptied himself
James 1:9-11 Poverty and riches
James 2:1-7 Respect for the poor
James 5:1-6 A warning for the rich
1 John 3:16-18 Seeing the needs of others
1 Timothy 6:6-10 The trap of riches
Hebrews 10:32-34 A lasting possession
Revelation 18:1-3; 9-15-24 Wealth is taken away

Tithing of Time

"Tithing of time" means being in actual direct contact with the poor, visiting with them, and/or getting involved in very simple service efforts, more elaborate projects or structural change programs. This may take up an hour or more a week, a day a month, a week a year or some longer period at other intervals. The purpose of "tithing of time" is to provide an opportunity to be with the poor so that they are not statistics but persons, not problems but friends.

Below are a few suggestions for ways in which our opting for the poor can be strengthened by "tithing of time."

1. Visit prisoners in local jails.
2. Assist newly-arrived refugees to find housing and jobs.
3. Volunteer at a home for battered women.
4. Assist in local soup kitchens.
5. Visit nursing homes for the elderly poor.
6. Repair homes of the poor.
7. Get involved in school social service

programs.

8. Take part in "Big Sisters/Brothers" programs.

9. Go shopping for the poor who lack transportation.

10. Help out in local night shelters for the homeless.

11. Teach English to migrant workers and refugees.

12. Visit the poor in public hospitals.

13. Visit police stations and courts to be with families of the poor who are in trouble.

14. Attend meetings of inner-city community organizations.

15. Tutor students in schools in poor neighborhoods.